Hamad Bin Khalifa University Press
P O Box 5825
Doha, Qatar

www.hbkupress.com

First published in Arabic by Hamad Bin Khalifa University Press, 2021.
Translation Copyright © Hamad Bin Khalifa University Press.

All rights reserved.

No part of this publication may be reproduced or transmitted in any form or by any means, electronic or mechanical, including photocopying, recording, or any information storage or retrieval system, without prior permission in writing from the publishers.

No responsibility for loss caused to any individual or organization acting on or refraining from action as a result of the material in this publication can be accepted by HBKU Press or the author.

First English edition, 2022

Hamad Bin Khalifa University Press

ISBN: 9789927161018

Printed in Doha-Qatar.

Qatar National Library Cataloging-in-Publication (CIP)

Elkhatib, Basma, author.

[حفلة ليان]. English

Layan's party / by Basma Elkhatib ; illustrations by Inna Ogando ; translated by Mohammad Ramadan. First English edition. – Doha, Qatar : Hamad Bin Khalifa University Press, 2022.

pages ; cm

ISBN 978-992-716-101-8

Translation of: حفلة ليان.

1. Children's stories, Arabic, Translations into English. 2. Picture books. I. Ogando, Inna, illustrator. II. Ramadan, Mohammad, translator. III. Title.

PZ10.731. K4313 2022
892.737– dc 23

20222838345x

LAYAN'S PARTY

By Basma Elkhatib

Illustrations by Inna Ogando

Translated by Mohammad Ramadan

In a couple of days, Layan will celebrate her birthday.
Layan is a little girl who loves celebrations and loves shopping for parties even more.

"I hope I get a cat for my birthday," she said out loud.
"But who would take care of it?" her mother asked.
Layan replied, "I'm ten years old now, I can take care of it myself."
Dad interrupted her. "A cat would be expensive to take care of ."
"I'll pay for her from my own allowance and savings," Layan insisted.

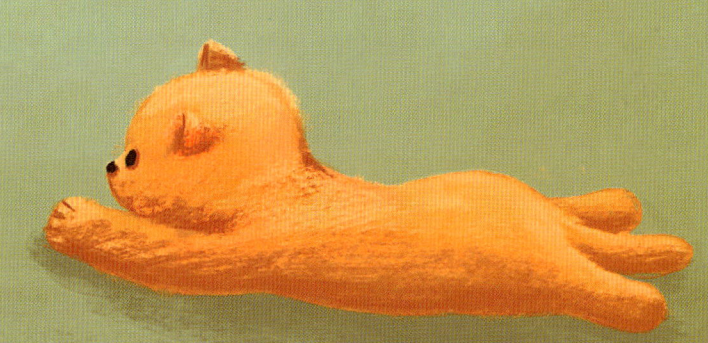

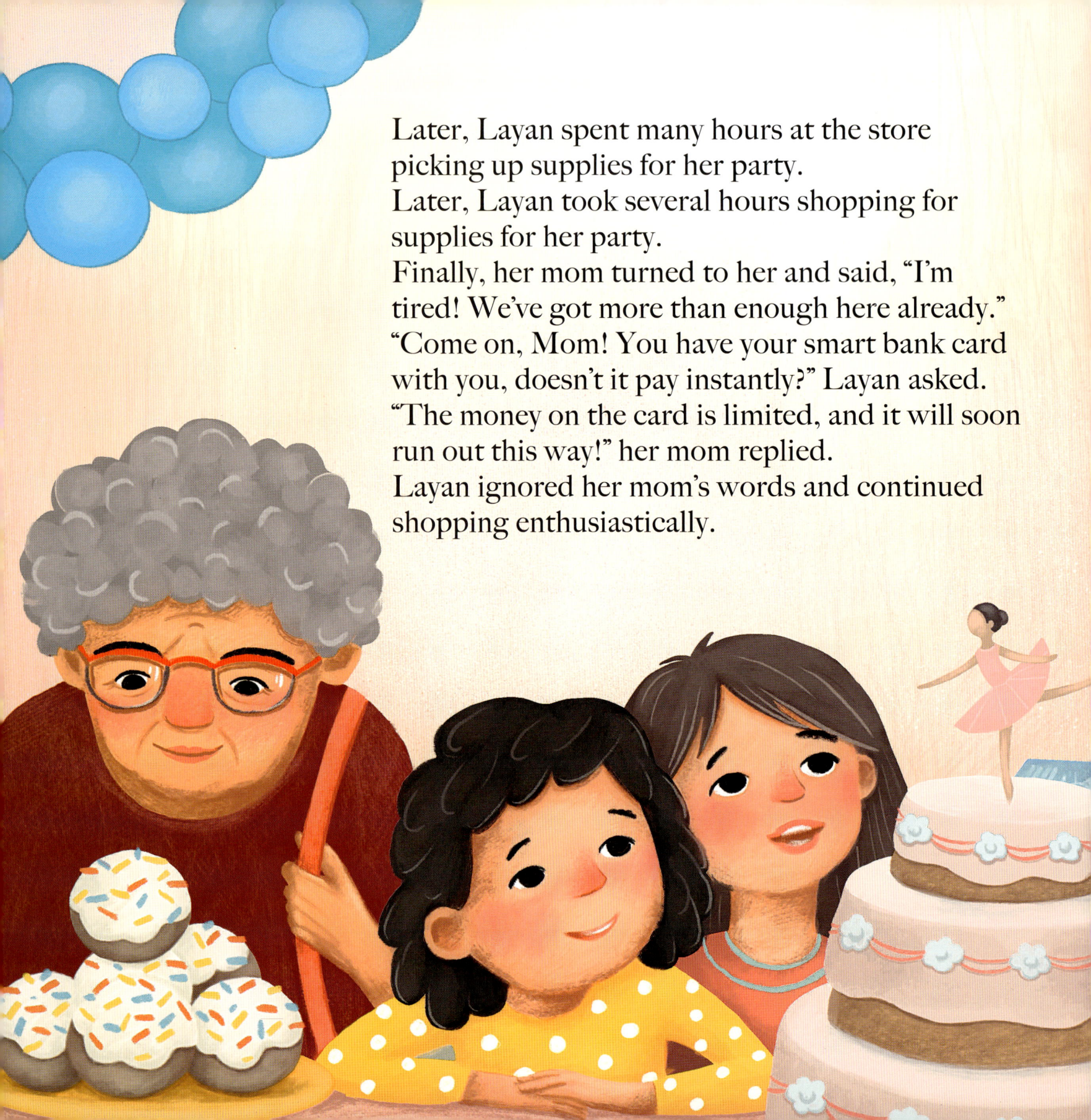

Later, Layan spent many hours at the store picking up supplies for her party.
Later, Layan took several hours shopping for supplies for her party.
Finally, her mom turned to her and said, "I'm tired! We've got more than enough here already."
"Come on, Mom! You have your smart bank card with you, doesn't it pay instantly?" Layan asked.
"The money on the card is limited, and it will soon run out this way!" her mom replied.
Layan ignored her mom's words and continued shopping enthusiastically.

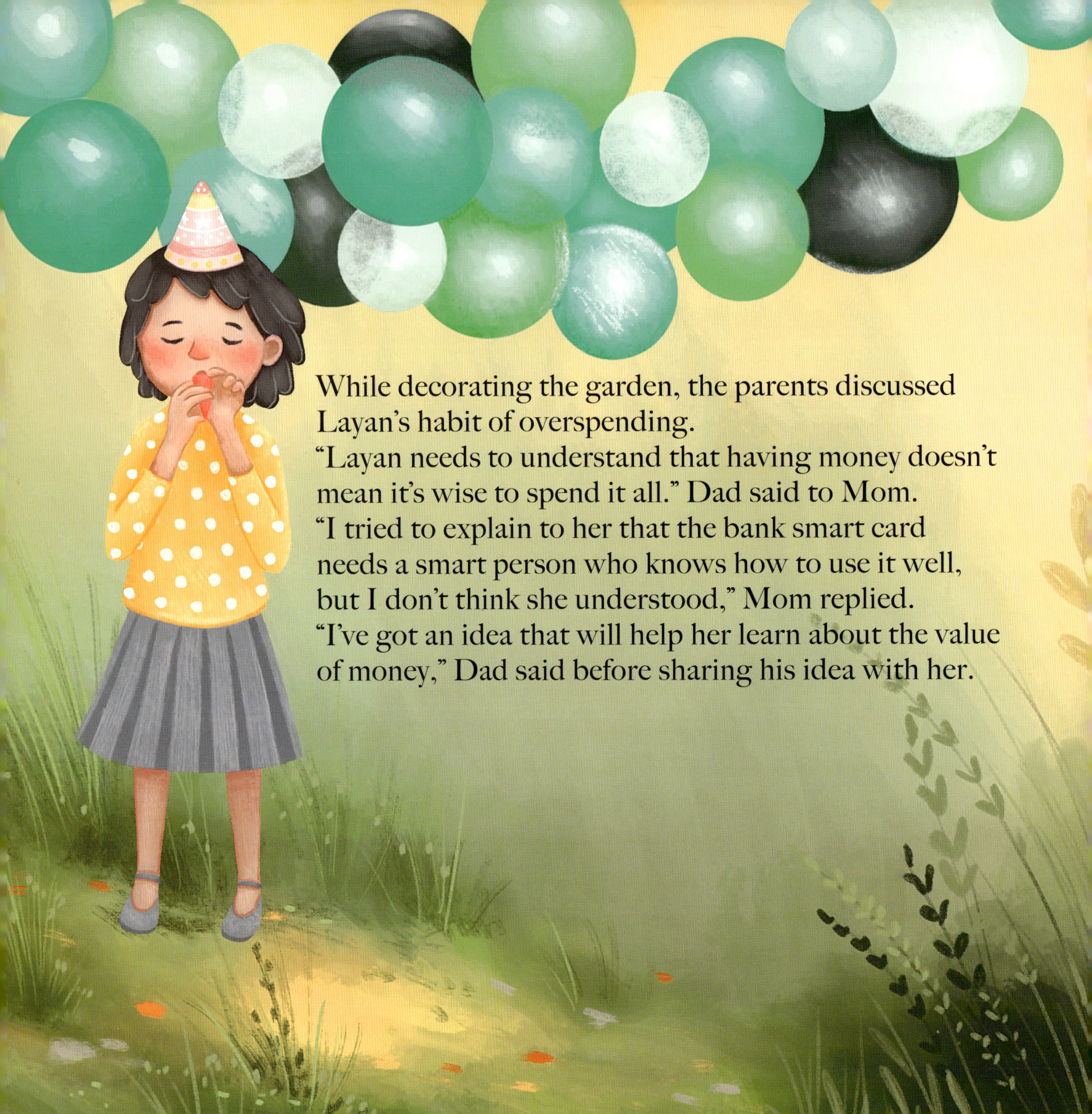

While decorating the garden, the parents discussed Layan's habit of overspending.
"Layan needs to understand that having money doesn't mean it's wise to spend it all." Dad said to Mom.
"I tried to explain to her that the bank smart card needs a smart person who knows how to use it well, but I don't think she understood," Mom replied.
"I've got an idea that will help her learn about the value of money," Dad said before sharing his idea with her.

Layan's party was in full swing when it was finally time to open presents.

Dad presented Layan with a colored box, saying, "My lovely daughter, I wish you a long and happy life. This present is from me and your mom."

Enthusiastically, Layan opened the box. "A cat! A cat! I've been wishing for one for years!" she shouted joyfully.

Layan thanked her parents excitedly and skipped to the garden with her cat, whom she named "Caty".

Once the guests left, Layan and her family began collecting the huge amounts of leftovers.
"Didn't I tell you, Layan, that we bought much more than our needs?" her mother said.
"Could we resell this food and make our money back?" Layan asked.
"No. You and I will go out and offer it to people in need," Mom replied.

"But I want to play with my cat, and show her where to sleep, and…"
Mom interrupted her. "Not until you tidy the place and distribute the food. You were the one who bought so much."

The next day, Layan went to the bank with her dad, where she deposited the money she had been saving all year. She also received a card to pay with.

"Pay attention to how you spend money," Dad warned. "If you don't take care of the cat, I'll send it back to the pet shelter."

"I'll take care of it, Dad. I'll handle everything!" responded Layan confidently.

At the pet store, Layan bought cat food, a cat bed to keep in her room, another bed for naps out in the hall, a lot of balls, and ribbons in every color of the rainbow.

"Do you know how much all this stuff is?" Dad asked her before she could pay.

"Almost. Don't worry, Dad. I have enough money," she replied.

Layan paid. A big amount was drawn out of her account, but she did not care.

Next, Layan took her cat to the vet.
The vet gave the cat the required vaccines and asked Layan to bring it next month for a follow up.
Layan paid the vet's fees and the vaccines' costs.
Even more money was drawn out of her account.

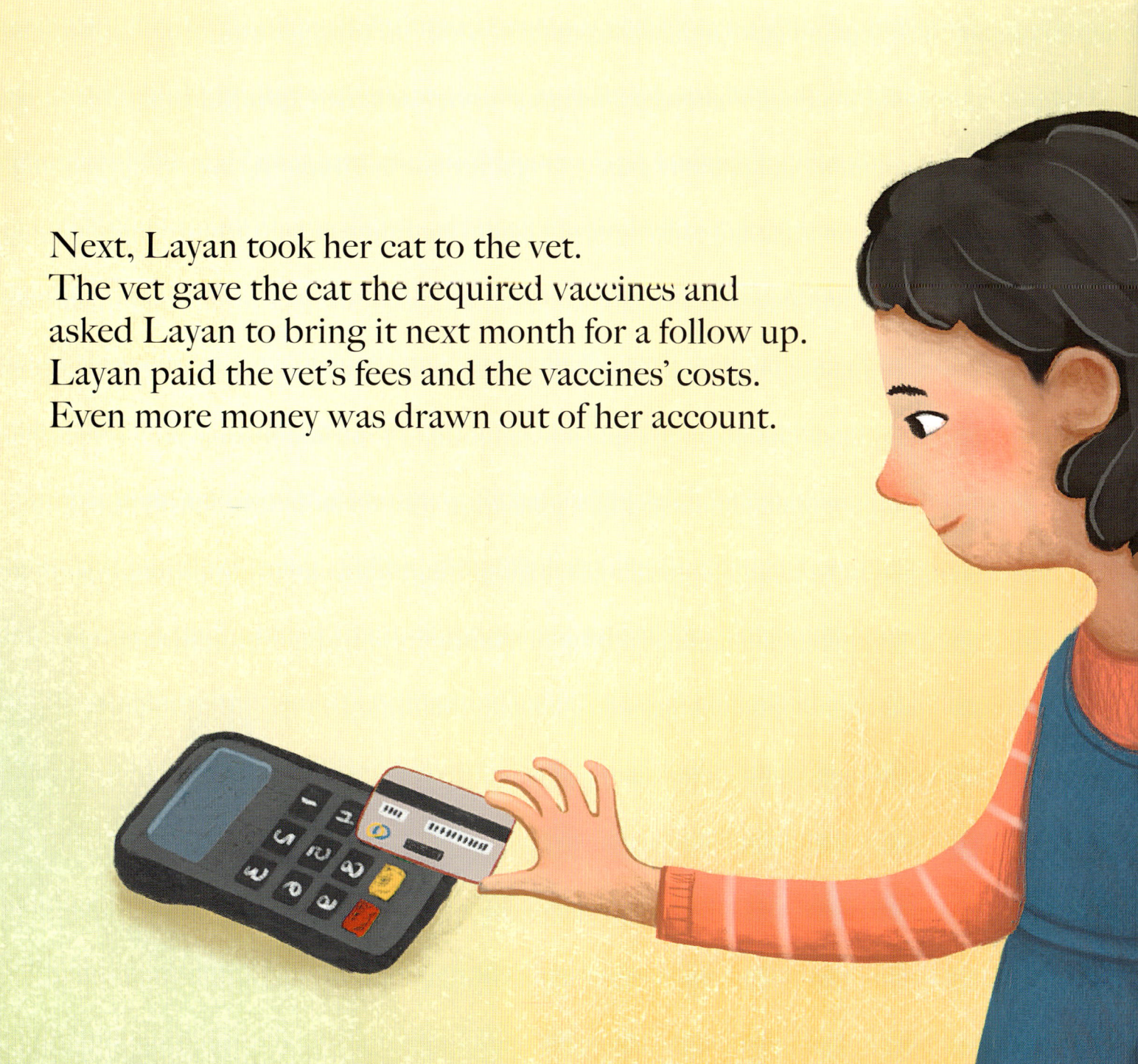

Days later, Caty fell ill.
She got tired and lost her appetite.

Again, Layan brought it to the vet.
"Your cat is sick, and it needs medicine and special food," the vet said after examining her.

Layan paid the vet's fees, then went to the pharmacy to buy the medicine and food.

But then, something bad happened at the pharmacy.
Layan's card ran out of money!
Layan was shocked, and very worried about her cat!
If Caty does not get the right treatment, she'll get even sicker.
"If only I had bought just what Caty needed, and not wasted so much!" Layan cried anxiously.
Dad interfered saying, "I'll give you your monthly allowance early today, as long as you promise to make it last until the end of the month."
Layan agreed to her dad's offer.
She paid for the medicine and deposited the rest of her allowance into her bank account.

A week later, Caty recovered. Caty started playing and having fun again!
Omar, Layan's brother, suggested that she celebrate Caty's recovery. Layan welcomed the idea.
Omar brought his sister a notebook and a pen to list everything she would need. "Milk, cornstarch, cinnamon and honey," Layan said simply.
"What's this?" Omar interrupted in wonder.
"This is exactly what we need to make pudding and celebrate in our garden, already decorated with pretty flowers," Layan replied.

Layan served the pudding to her family - and her cat, too! Astonished, her brother said, "But you have money and can buy plenty of desserts."
"That money is for important things, like Caty's vaccines and medicine if she gets sick again. Buying more is just careless spending," she responded.
"Careless spending?" echoed Omar.

"Yes, careless spending is to spend money irresponsibly, and it can have really bad consequences. I learned to be smarter than the smart cards," Layan told her brother. The parents smiled, pleased with their daughter's words.

"You know, there are a lot of cats out there in need of care," said Omar.

"Well, just one cat is enough for me!" Layan laughed.